The Raven

Also Illustrated by Alan James Robinson:

THE JUMPING FROG by Mark Twain

THE BLACK CAT by Edgar Allan Poe

THE RAVEN

with THE PHILOSOPHY OF COMPOSITION

Edgar Allan Poe

Wood Engravings by Alan James Robinson

MOYER BELL
Wakefield, Rhode Island & London

Published by Moyer Bell

The Raven is copyright © 1986 by Press of the Sea Turtle. Text is
the original 1845 Lorimer Graham version with author's corrections.
Reprinted 1996 by arrangement with Press of the Sea Turtle.

The Philosophy of Composition was originally published in Graham's
Magazine in April 1846.

First Edition

LIBRARY OF CONGRESS
CATALOGING-IN-PUBLICATION DATA

Poe, Edgar Allan, 1809–1849.
        The raven with : The philosophy of composition.
        p.   cm.
        I. Title. II. Philosophy of composition.
        PS2609.AI   1996
        811'.3   86-12475
                           CIP
ISBN 1-55921-178-4 (alk.paper)

Printed in the United States of America
Distributed in North America by
Publishers Group West, P.O. Box 8843, Emeryville CA 94662
800-788-3123 (in California 510-658-3453).

The Raven

Once upon a midnight dreary, while I pondered, weak and weary,
Over many a quaint and curious volume of forgotten lore—
While I nodded, nearly napping, suddenly there came a tapping,
As of some one gently rapping, rapping at my chamber door.
" 'Tis some visitor," I muttered, "tapping at my chamber door—
                              Only this and nothing more."

Ah, distinctly I remember it was in the bleak December;
And each separate dying ember wrought its ghost upon the floor.
Eagerly I wished the morrow;—vainly I had sought to borrow
From my books surcease of sorrow—sorrow for the lost Lenore—
For the rare and radiant maiden whom the angels name Lenore—
                              Nameless *here* for evermore.

And the silken, sad, uncertain rustling of each purple curtain
Thrilled me—filled me with fantastic terrors never felt before;
So that now, to still the beating of my heart, I stood repeating
" 'Tis some visitor entreating entrance at my chamber door—
Some late visitor entreating entrance at my chamber door;—
                                        This it is and nothing more."

Presently my soul grew stronger; hesitating then no longer,
"Sir," said I, "or Madam, truly your forgiveness I implore;
But the fact is I was napping, and so gently you came rapping,
And so faintly you came tapping, tapping at my chamber door,
That I scarce was sure I heard you"—here I opened wide the door;—
                                        Darkness there and nothing more.

Deep into that darkness peering, long I stood there wondering, fearing,
Doubting, dreaming dreams no mortal ever dared to dream before;
But the silence was unbroken, and the stillness gave no token,
And the only word there spoken was the whispered word, "Lenore?"
This I whispered, and an echo murmured back the word "Lenore!"
                                        Merely this and nothing more.

Back into the chamber turning, all my soul within me burning,
Soon again I heard a tapping somewhat louder than before.
"Surely," said I, "surely that is something at my window lattice;
Let me see, then, what thereat is, and this mystery explore—
Let my heart be still a moment and this mystery explore;—
                                        'Tis the wind and nothing more!"

Open here I flung the shutter, when, with many a flirt and flutter,
In there stepped a stately Raven of the saintly days of yore;
Not the least obeisance made he; not a minute stopped or stayed he;
But, with mien of lord or lady, perched above my chamber door—
Perched upon a bust of Pallas just above my chamber door—
                              Perched, and sat, and nothing more.

Then this ebony bird beguiling my sad fancy into smiling,
By the grave and stern decorum of the countenance it wore,
"Though thy crest be shorn & shaven, thou," I said, "art sure no craven,
Ghastly grim and ancient Raven wandering from the Nightly shore—
Tell me what thy lordly name is on the Night's Plutonian shore!"
                              Quoth the Raven, "Nevermore."

Much I marvelled this ungainly fowl to hear discourse so plainly,
Though its answer little meaning—little relevancy bore;
For we cannot help agreeing that no living human being
Ever yet was blessed with seeing bird above his chamber door—
Bird or beast upon the sculptured bust above his chamber door,
                                        With such name as "Nevermore."

But the Raven, sitting lonely on the placid bust, spoke only
That one word, as if his soul in that one word he did outpour.
Nothing further then he uttered—not a feather then he fluttered—
Till I scarcely more than muttered "Other friends have flown before—
On the morrow *he* will leave me, as my Hopes have flown before."
                                        Then the bird said, "Nevermore."

Startled at the stillness broken by reply so aptly spoken,
"Doubtless," said I, "what it utters is its only stock and store
Caught from some unhappy master whom unmerciful Disaster
Followed fast and followed faster till his songs one burden bore—
Till the dirges of his Hope that melancholy burden bore
                              Of 'Never—nevermore.' "

But the Raven still beguiling all my fancy into smiling,
Straight I wheeled a cushioned seat in front of bird, and bust and door;
Then, upon the velvet sinking, I betook myself to linking
Fancy unto fancy, thinking what this ominous bird of yore—
What this grim, ungainly, ghastly, gaunt and ominous bird of yore
                              Meant in croaking "Nevermore."

This I sat engaged in guessing, but no syllable expressing
To the fowl whose fiery eyes now burned into my bosom's core;
This and more I sat divining, with my head at ease reclining
On the cushion's velvet lining that the lamp-light gloated o'er,
But whose velvet-violet lining with the lamp-light gloating o'er,
                      She shall press, ah, nevermore!

Then, methought, the air grew denser, perfumed from an unseen censer
Swung by Seraphim whose foot-falls tinkled on the tufted floor.
"Wretch," I cried, "thy God hath lent thee—by these angels he hath sent thee
Respite—respite and nepenthe from thy memories of Lenore;
Quaff, oh, quaff this kind nepenthe and forget this lost Lenore!"
                      Quoth the Raven, "Nevermore."

"Prophet!" said I, "thing of evil!—prophet still, if bird or devil!—
Whether Tempter sent, or whether tempest tossed thee here ashore,
Desolate yet all undaunted, on this desert land enchanted—
On this home by Horror haunted—tell me truly, I implore—
Is there—*is* there balm in Gilead?—tell me—tell me, I implore!"
                    Quoth the Raven, "Nevermore."

"Prophet!" said I, "thing of evil!—prophet still, if bird or devil!
By that Heaven that bends above us—by that God we both adore—
Tell this soul with sorrow laden if, within the distant Aidenn,
It shall clasp the sainted maiden whom the angels name Lenore—
Clasp a rare and radiant maiden whom the angels name Lenore."
                    Quoth the Raven, "Nevermore."

"Be that word our sin of parting, bird or fiend!" I shrieked, upstarting—
"Get thee back into the tempest and the Night's Plutonian shore!
Leave no black plume as a token of that lie thy soul hath spoken!
Leave my loneliness unbroken!—quit the bust above my door!
Take thy beak from out my heart, and take thy form from off my door!"
                              Quoth the Raven, "Nevermore."

And the Raven, never flitting, still is sitting, *still* is sitting
On the pallid bust of Pallas just above my chamber door;
And his eyes have all the seeming of a demon's that is dreaming,
And the lamp-light o'er him streaming throws his shadow on the floor;
And my soul from out that shadow that lies floating on the floor
                              Shall be lifted—nevermore!

The Philosophy of Composition

CHARLES DICKENS, in a note now lying before me, alluding to an examination I once made of the mechanism of *Barnaby Rudge*, says: "By the way, are you aware that Godwin wrote his *Caleb Williams* backward? He first involved his hero in a web of difficulties, forming the second volume, and then, for the first, cast about him for some mode of accounting for what had been done."

I cannot think this the precise mode of procedure on the part of Godwin, and indeed what he himself acknowledges is not altogether in accordance with Mr. Dickens's idea; but the author of *Caleb Williams* was too good an artist not to perceive the advantage derivable from at least a somewhat similar process. Nothing is more clear than that every plot, worth the name, must be elaborated to its *dénouement* before anything be attempted with the pen. It is only with the *dénouement* constantly in view that we can give a plot its indispensable air of consequence, or causation, by making the incidents, and especially the tone at all points, tend to the development of the intention.

There is a radical error, I think, in the usual mode of constructing a story. Either history affords a thesis, or one is suggested by an incident of the day, or, at best, the author sets himself to work in the combination of striking events to form merely the basis of his narrative, designing, generally, to fill in with description, dialogue, or authorial comment, whatever crevices of fact or action may, from page to page, render themselves apparent.

I prefer commencing with the consideration of an effect. Keeping originality always in view,—for he is false to himself who ventures to dispense with so obvious and so easily attainable a source of interest,—I say to myself, in the first place: "Of the innumerable effects, or impressions, of which the heart, the intellect, or (more generally) the soul is susceptible, what one shall I, on the present occasion, select?" Having chosen a novel, first, and secondly a vivid effect, I consider whether it can be best wrought by incident or tone,—whether by ordinary incidents and peculiar tone, or the converse, or by peculiarity both of incident and tone; afterward looking about me, or rather within, for such combinations of event, or tone, as shall best aid me in the construction of the effect.

I have often thought how interesting a magazine paper might be written by any author who would, that is to say, who could, detail, step by step, the processes by which any one of his compositions attained its ultimate point of completion. Why such a paper has never been given to the world I am much at a loss to say, but perhaps the authorial vanity has had more to do with the omission than any one other cause. Most writers, poets in especial, prefer having it understood that they compose by a species of fine frenzy, an ecstatic intuition, and would positively shudder at letting the public take a peep behind the scenes at the elaborate and vacillating crudities of thought; at the true purposes seized only at the last moment; at the innumerable glimpses of idea that arrived not at the maturity of full view; at the full matured fancies discarded in despair as unmanageable; at the cautious selections and rejections; at the painful erasures and interpolations,—in a word, at the wheels and pinions, the tackle for scene-shifting, the step-ladders and demon-traps, the cock's feathers, the red paint and the black patches which, in ninety-nine cases out of the hundred, constitute the properties of the literary *histrio*.

I am aware, on the other hand, that the case is by no means common in which an author is at all in condition to retrace the steps by which his conclusions have been attained. In general, suggestions, having arisen pell-mell, are pursued and forgotten in a similar manner.

For my own part, I have neither sympathy with the repugnance alluded to, nor, at any time, the least difficulty in recalling to mind the progressive steps of any of my compositions; and, since the interest of an analysis, or reconstruction, such as I have considered a desideratum, is quite independent of any real or fancied interest in the thing analyzed, it will not be regarded as a breach of decorum on my part to show the *modus operandi* by which some one of my own works was put together. I select *The Raven* as most generally known. It is my design to render it manifest that no one point in its composition is referable either to accident or intuition, that the work proceeded, step by step, to its completion with the precision and rigid consequence of a mathematical problem.

Let us dismiss, as irrelevant to the poem *per se*, the circumstance, or say the necessity, which, in the first place, gave rise to the intention of composing a poem that should suit at once the popular and the critical taste.

We commence, then, with this intention.

The initial consideration was that of extent. If any literary work is too long to be read at one sitting, we must be content to dispense with the immensely important effect derivable from unity of impression; for, if two sittings be required, the affairs of the world interfere, and everything like totality is at once destroyed.

But since, *ceteris paribus*, no poet can afford to dispense with anything that may advance his design, it but remains to be seen whether there is, in extent, any advantage to counterbalance the loss of unity which attends it. Here I say no, at once. What we term a long poem is, in fact, merely a succession of brief ones; that is to say, of brief poetical effects. It is needless to demonstrate that a poem is such, only inasmuch as it intensely excites, by elevating, the soul; and all intense excitements are, through a physical necessity, brief. For this reason, at least one half of the *Paradise Lost* is essentially prose, a succession of poetical excitements interspersed, inevitably, with corresponding depressions, the whole being deprived, through the extremeness of its length, of the vastly important artistic element, totality, or unity, of effect.

It appears evident, then, that there is a distinct limit, as regards length, to all works of literary art—the limit of a single sitting—and that, although in certain classes of prose composition, such as *Robinson Crusoe* (demanding no unity), this limit may be advantageously overpassed, it can never properly be overpassed in a poem. Wirhin this limit, the extent of a poem may be made to bear mathematical relation to its merit; in other words, to the excitement or elevation; again, in other words, to the degree of the true poetical effect which it is capable of inducing; for it is clear that the brevity must be in direct ratio of the intensity of the intended effect:—this, with one proviso, that a certain degree of duration is absolutely requisite for the production of any effect at all.

Holding in view these considerations, as well as that degree of excitement which I deemed not above the popular, while not below the critical, taste, I reached at once what I conceived the proper length for my intended poem, a length of about one hundred lines. It is, in fact, a hundred and eight.

My next thought concerned the choice of an impression, or effect, to be conveyed; and here I may as well observe that, throughout the construction, I kept steadily in view the design of rendering the work universally appreciable. I should be carried too far out of my immediate topic were I to demonstrate a point upon which I have repeatedly insisted, and which, with the poetical, stands not in the slightest need of demonstration—the point, I mean, that beauty is the sole legitimate province of the poem. A few words, however, in elucidation of my real meaning, which some of my friends have evinced a disposition to misrepresent. That pleasure which is at once the most intense, the most elevating, and the most pure, is, I believe, found in the contemplation of the beautiful. When, indeed, men speak of beauty, they mean, precisely, not a quality, as is supposed, but an effect; they refer, in short, just to that intense and pure elevation of soul, not of intellect or of heart, upon which I have commented, and which is experienced in consequence of contemplating "the beautiful." Now I designate beauty as the province of the poem, merely because it is an obvious rule of art that effects should be made to spring from direct causes, that objects should be attained through means best adapted for their attainment, no one as yet having been weak enough to deny that the peculiar elevation alluded to is most readily attained in the poem. Now the object, truth, or the satisfaction of the intellect, and the object, passion, or the excitement of the heart, are, although attainable to a certain extent in poetry, far more readily attainable in prose. Truth, in fact, demands a precision, and passion a homeliness (the truly passionate will comprehend me), which are absolutely antagonistic to that beauty which, I maintain, is the excitement, or pleasurable elevation, of the soul. It by no means follows from anything here said, that passion, or even truth, may not be introduced, and even profitably introduced, into a poem, for they may serve in elucidation, or aid the general effect, as do discords in music, by contrast; but the true artist will always contrive, first, to tone them into proper subservience to the predominant aim, and, secondly, to enveil them, as far as possible, in that beauty which is the atmosphere and the essence of the poem.

Regarding, then, beauty as my province, my next question referred to the tone of its highest manifestation, and all experience has shown that this tone is one of sadness. Beauty of whatever kind, in its supreme development, invariably excites the sensitive soul to tears. Melancholy is thus the most legitimate of all the poetical tones.

The length, the province, and the tone, being thus determined, I betook myself to ordinary induction, with the view of obtaining some artistic piquancy which might serve me as a key-note in the construction of the poem, some pivot upon which the whole structure might turn. In carefully thinking over all the usual artistic effects, or, more properly, points, in the theatrical sense, I did not fail to perceive immediately that no one had been so universally employed as that of the refrain. The universality of its employment sufficed to assure me of its intrinsic value, and spared me the necessity of submitting it to analysis. I considered it, however, with regard to its susceptibility of improvement, and soon saw it to be in a primitive condition. As commonly used, the refrain, or burden, not only is limited to lyric verse, but depends for its impression upon the force of monotone, both in sound and thought. The pleasure is deduced solely from the sense of identity—of repetition. I resolved to diversify, and so heighten, the effect, by adhering, in general, to the monotone of sound, while I continually varied that of thought: that is to say, I determined to produce continuously novel effects, by the variation of the application of the refrain, the refrain itself remaining, for the most part, unvaried.

These points being settled, I next bethought me of the nature of my refrain. Since its application was to be repeatedly varied, it was clear that the refrain itself must be brief, for there would have been an insurmountable difficulty in frequent variations of application in any sentence of length. In proportion to the brevity of the sentence, would, of course, be the facility of the variation. This led me at once to a single word as the best refrain.

The question now arose as to the character of the word. Having made up my mind to a refrain, the division of the poem into stanzas was, of course, a corollary, the refrain forming the close to each stanza. That such a close, to have force, must be sonorous and susceptible of protracted emphasis admitted no doubt; and these considerations inevitably led me to the long "o" as the most sonorous vowel, in connection with "r" as the most producible consonant.

The sound of the refrain being thus determined, it became necessary to select a word embodying this sound, and at the same time in the fullest possible keeping with that melancholy which I had predetermined as the tone of the poem. In such a search it would have been absolutely impossible to overlook the word "Nevermore." In fact, it was the very first which presented itself.

The next desideratum was a pretext for the continuous use of the one word "Nevermore." In observing the difficulty which I at once found in inventing a sufficiently plausible reason for its continuous repetition, I did not fail to perceive that this difficulty arose solely from the pre-assumption that the word was to be so continuously or monotonously spoken by a human being; I did not fail to perceive, in short, that the difficulty lay in the reconciliation of this monotony with the exercise of reason on the part of the creature repeating the word. Here, then, immediately arose the idea of a non-reasoning creature capable of speech; and, very naturally, a parrot, in the first instance, suggested itself, but was superseded forthwith by a Raven, as equally capable of speech, and infinitely more in keeping with the intended tone.

I had now gone so far as the conception of a Raven, the bird of ill omen, monotonously repeating the one word, "Nevermore," at the conclusion of each stanza, in a poem of melancholy tone, and in length about one hundred lines. Now, never losing sight of the object, supremeness, or perfection, at all points, I asked myself: "Of all melancholy topics, what, according to the universal understanding of mankind, is the most melancholy?" "Death" was the obvious reply. "And when," I said, "is this most melancholy of topics most poetical?" From what I have already explained at some length, the answer here, also, is obvious: "When it most closely allies itself to beauty: the death, then of a beautiful woman is, unquestionably, the most poetical topic in the world; and equally is it beyond doubt that the lips best suited for such topic are those of a bereaved lover."

I had now to combine the two ideas, of a lover lamenting his deceased mistress and a Raven continuously repeating the word "Nevermore." I had to combine these, bearing in mind my design of varying, at every turn, the application of the word repeated; but the only intelligible mode of such combination is that of imagining the Raven employing the word in answer to the queries of the lover. And here it was that I saw at once the opportunity afforded for the effect on which I had been depending; that is to say, the effect of the variation of application. I saw that I could make the first query propounded by the lover the first query to which the

Raven should reply "Nevermore," that I could make this first query a common-place one; the second less so, the third still less, and so on, until at length the lover, startled from his original nonchalance by the melancholy character of the word itself, by its frequent repetition, and by a consideration of the ominous reputation of the fowl that uttered it, is at length excited to superstition, and wildly pro-pounds queries of a far different character,—queries whose solution he has pas-sionately at heart,—propounds them half in superstition and half in that species of despair which delights in self-torture; propounds them not altogether because he believes in the prophetic or demoniac character of the bird (which, reason assures him, is merely repeating a lesson learned by rote), but because he experiences a frenzied pleasure in so modelling his questions as to receive from the expected "Nevermore" the most delicious because the most intolerable of sorrow. Per-ceiving the opportunity thus afforded me, or, more strictly, thus forced upon me in the progress of the construction, I first established in mind the climax, or con-cluding query—that query to which "Nevermore" should be in the last place an answer; that query in reply to which this word "Nevermore" should involve the utmost conceivable amount of sorrow and despair.

Here, then, the poem may be said to have its beginning—at the end, where all works of art should begin; for it was here, at this point of my preconsiderations, that I first put pen to paper in the composition of the stanza:

"Prophet," said I, "thing of evil! prophet still, if bird or devil!
By that heaven that bends above us, by that God we both adore,
Tell this soul with sorrow laden if, within the distant Aidenn,

It shall clasp a sainted maiden whom the angels name Lenore,
Clasp a rare and radiant maiden whom the angels name Lenore."
                    Quoth the Raven, "Nevermore."

I composed this stanza, at this point, first that, by establishing the climax, I might the better vary and graduate, as regards seriousness and importance, the preceding queries of the lover; and, secondly, that I might definitely settle the rhythm, the metre, and the length and general arrangement of the stanzas, as well as graduate the stanzas which were to precede, so that none of them might surpass this in rhythmical effect. Had I been able, in the subsequent composition, to construct more vigorous stanzas, I should, without scruple, have purposely enfeebled them, so as not to interfere with the climacteric effect.

And here I may as well say a few words of the versification. My first object, as usual, was originality. The extent to which this has been neglected in versification is one of the most unaccountable things in the world. Admitting that there is little possibility of variety in mere rhythm, it is still clear that the possible varieties of metre and stanza are absolutely infinite; and yet, for centuries, no man, in verse, has ever done, or ever seemed to think of doing, an original thing. The fact is, that originality, unless in minds of very unusual force, is by no means a matter, as some suppose, of impulse or intuition. In general, to be found, it must be elaborately sought, and although a positive merit of the highest class, demands in its attainment less of invention than negation.

Of course, I pretend to no originality in either the rhythm or metre of *The Raven*. The former is trochaic; the latter is octameter acatalectic, alternating with heptameter catalectic repeated in the refrain of the fifth verse, and terminating with tetrameter catalectic. Less pedantically, the feet employed throughout (trochees) consist of a long syllable followed by a short: the first line of the stanza consists of eight of these feet; the second of seven and a half (in effect two thirds); the third of eight; the fourth of seven and a half; the fifth the same; the sixth three and a half. Now, each of these lines, taken individually, has been employed before, and what originality *The Raven* has, is in their combination into stanza; nothing even remotely approaching this combination has ever been attempted. The effect of this originality of combination is aided by other unusual and some altogether novel effects, arising from an extension of the application of the principles of rhyme and alliteration.

The next point to be considered was the mode of bringing together the lover and the Raven, and the first branch of this consideration was the locale. For this the most natural suggestion might seem to be a forest or the fields, but it has always appeared to me that a close circumscription of space is absolutely necessary to the effect of insulated incident: it has the force of a frame to a picture. It has an indisputable moral power in keeping concentrated the attention, and, of course, must not be confounded with mere unity of place.

I determined, then, to place the lover in his chamber,—in a chamber rendered sacred to him by memories of her who had frequented it. The room is represented as richly furnished; this, in mere pursuance of the ideas I have already explained on the subject of beauty as the sole true poetical thesis.

The locale being thus determined, I had now to introduce the bird, and the thought of introducing him through the window was inevitable. The idea of making the lover suppose, in the first instance, that the flapping of the wings of the bird against the shutter is a "tapping" at the door originated in a wish to increase, by prolonging, the reader's curiosity, and in a desire to admit the incidental effect arising from the lover's throwing open the door, finding all dark, and thence adopting the half-fancy that it was the spirit of his mistress that knocked.

I made the night tempestuous, first, to account for the Raven's seeking admission, and, secondly, for the effect of contrast with the physical serenity within the chamber.

I made the bird alight on the bust of Pallas, also for the effect of contrast between the marble and the plumage,—it being understood that the bust was absolutely suggested by the bird; the bust of Pallas being chosen, first, as most in keeping with the scholarship of the lover, and, secondly, for the sonorousness of the word "Pallas" itself.

About the middle of the poem, also, I have availed myself of the force of contrast, with a view of deepening the ultimate impression. For example, an air of the fantastic, approaching as nearly to the ludicrous as was admissible, is given to the Raven's entrance. He comes in "with many a flirt and flutter."

Not the *least obeisance made he;* not a moment stopped or stayed he,
But with *mien of lord or lady,* perched above my chamber door.

In the two stanzas which follow, the design is more obviously carried out:

Then this ebony bird beguiling my sad fancy into smiling,
By the *grave and stern decorum of the countenance it wore,*
"Though thy *crest be shorn and shaven,* thou," I said, "art sure no craven,

Ghastly grim and ancient Raven wandering from the nightly shore;
Tell me what thy lordly name is on the Night's Plutonian shore?''

> Quoth the Raven, ''Nevermore.''

Much I marvelled *this ungainly fowl* to hear discourse so plainly,
Though its answer little meaning, little relevancy bore;
For we cannot help agreeing that no living human being
Ever yet was blest with seeing bird above his chamber door—
Bird or beast upon the sculptured bust above his chamber door,

> With such name as ''Nevermore.''

The effect of the *dénouement* being thus provided for, I immediately drop the fantastic for a tone of the most profound seriousness, this tone commencing in the stanza directly following the one last quoted, with the line,

But the Raven, sitting lonely on that placid bust, spoke only, etc.

From this epoch the lover no longer jests, no longer sees anything even of the fantastic in the Raven's demeanor. He speaks of him as a ''grim, ungainly, ghastly, gaunt, and ominous bird of yore,'' and feels the ''fiery eyes'' burning into his ''bosom's core.'' This revolution of thought, or fancy, on the lover's part is intended to induce a similar one on the part of the reader—to bring the mind into a proper frame for the *dénouement* which is now brought about as rapidly and as directly as possible.

With the *dénouement* proper—with the Raven's reply, ''Nevermore,'' to the lover's final demand if he shall meet his mistress in another world, the poem, in its obvious phase, that of a single narrative, may be said to have its completion. So far, everything is within the limits of the accountable, of the real. A Raven, having learned by rote the single word, "Nevermore," and having escaped from the custody of its owner, is driven at midnight, through the violence of a storm, to seek admission at a window from which a light still gleams,—the chamber-window of a student, occupied half in poring over a volume, half in dreaming over a beloved mistress deceased. The casement being thrown open at the fluttering of a bird's wings, the bird itself perches on the most convenient seat out of the immediate reach of the student, who, amused by the incident and the oddity of the visitor's demeanor, demands of it, in jest and without looking for a reply, its name. The Raven, addressed, answers with its customary word, "Nevermore," a word which finds immediate echo in the melancholy heart of the student, who, giving utterance aloud to certain thoughts suggested by the occasion, is again startled by the fowl's repetition of "Nevermore." The student now guesses the state of the case, but is impelled, as I have before explained, by the human thirst for self-torture, and in part by superstition, to propound such queries to the bird as will bring him, the lover, the most of the luxury of sorrow, through the anticipated answer, "Nevermore." With the indulgence, to the extreme, of this self-torture, the narration, in what I have termed its first or obvious phase, has a natural termination, and so far there has been no overstepping of the limits of the real.

But in subjects so handled, however skilfully, or with however vivid an array of incident, there is always a certain hardness or nakedness, which repels the artistical eye. Two things are invariably required: first, some amount of complexity, or more properly, adaptation; and, secondly, some amount of suggestiveness, some undercurrent, however indefinite, of meaning. It is this latter, in especial, which imparts to a work of art so much of that richness (to borrow from colloquy a forcible term) which we are too fond of confounding with the ideal. It is the excess of the suggested meaning, it is the rendering this the upper- instead of the under-current of the theme, which turns into prose (and that of the very flattest kind) the so-called poetry of the so-called transcendentalists.

Holding these opinions, I added the two concluding stanzas of the poem, their suggestiveness being thus made to pervade all the narrative which has preceded them. The under-current of meaning is rendered first apparent in the lines,

"Take thy beak from out *my heart*, and take thy form from off my door;"
                              Quoth the Raven, "Nevermore!"

It will be observed that the words, "from out my heart," involve the first metaphorical expression in the poem. They, with the answer, "Nevermore," dispose the mind to seek a moral in all that has been previously narrated. The reader begins now to regard the Raven as emblematical, but it is not until the very last line of the very last stanza that the intention of making him emblematical of mournful and never-ending remembrance is permitted distinctly to be seen:

And the Raven, never flitting, still is sitting, still is sitting
On the pallid bust of Pallas just above my chamber door;
And his eyes have all the seeming of a demon's that is dreaming,
And the lamplight o'er him streaming throws his shadow on the floor;
And my soul *from out that shadow* that lies floating on the floor
                              Shall be lifted—nevermore.

COLOPHON

THE RAVEN by Edgar Allan Poe was
designed by Alan James Robinson for
the Cheloniidae Press edition. The text
is the orginal 1845 Lorimer Graham
version with the author's corrections.
Eight wood engravings and an etching
are by Alan James Robinson. The
Monotype Centaur was set by
Mackenzie-Harris of San Francisco
except for this and the first four pages
of the book which were set by Alabama
Book Composition of Deatsville, Ala-
bama. The paper is an acid-free sheet.
The book was printed by Data Repro-
duction, Rochester Hills, Michigan.